Dear Parent:

Congratulations! Your child is taking the first steps on an exciting journey. The destination? Independent reading!

STEP INTO READING® will help your child get there. The program offers five steps to reading success. Each step includes fun stories and colorful art. There are also Step into Reading Sticker Books, Step into Reading Math Readers, Step into Reading Phonics Readers, Step into Reading Write-In Readers, and Step into Reading Phonics Boxed Sets—a complete literacy program with something to interest every child.

Learning to Read, Step by Step!

Ready to Read   Preschool–Kindergarten
• big type and easy words • rhyme and rhythm • picture clues
For children who know the alphabet and are eager to begin reading.

Reading with Help   Preschool–Grade 1
• basic vocabulary • short sentences • simple stories
For children who recognize familiar words and sound out new words with help.

Reading on Your Own   Grades 1–3
• engaging characters • easy-to-follow plots • popular topics
For children who are ready to read on their own.

Reading Paragraphs   Grades 2–3
• challenging vocabulary • short paragraphs • exciting stories
For newly independent readers who read simple sentences with confidence.

Ready for Chapters   Grades 2–4
• chapters • longer paragraphs • full-color art
For children who want to take the plunge into chapter books but still like colorful pictures.

STEP INTO READING® is designed to give every child a successful reading experience. The grade levels are only guides. Children can progress through the steps at their own speed, developing confidence in their reading, no matter what their grade.

Remember, a lifetime love of reading starts with a single step!

Step into Reading, Random House, and the Random House colophon are registered trademarks of
Random House, Inc.

Based in part on *The Cat in the Hat Knows a Lot About That!* TV series (Episode 5)
© CITH Productions, Inc. (a subsidiary of Portfolio Entertainment, Inc.), and Red Hat Animation, Ltd.
(a subsidiary of Collingwood O'Hare Productions, Ltd.), 2010–2011.

THE CAT IN THE HAT KNOWS A LOT ABOUT THAT! logo and word mark TM 2010 Dr. Seuss Enterprises,
L.P., Portfolio Entertainment, Inc., and Collingwood O'Hare Productions, Ltd. All rights reserved.
The PBS KIDS logo is a registered trademark of PBS. Both are used with permission.
All rights reserved.

Broadcast in Canada by Treehouse™. Treehouse™ is a trademark of the Corus® Entertainment Inc.
group of companies. All rights reserved.

Visit us on the Web!
StepIntoReading.com
Seussville.com
pbskids.org/catinthehat
treehousetv.com

Educators and librarians, for a variety of teaching tools, visit us at
www.randomhouse.com/teachers

Library of Congress Cataloging-in-Publication Data
Rabe, Tish.
Now you see me / by Tish Rabe ; based on a television script by Katherine Standford ;
illustrated by Christopher Moroney.
   p. cm. — (Step into reading. Step 2)
"Based in part on The Cat in the Hat Knows a Lot About That!"
ISBN 978-0-375-86706-4 (trade) — ISBN 978-0-375-96706-1 (lib. bdg.)
I. Standford, Katherine. II. Moroney, Christopher, ill. III. Cat in the hat knows a lot about that!
(Television program). IV. Title.
PZ8.3.R1145Now 2011 [E]—dc22 2009051723

Printed in the United States of America
10 9 8 7 6 5 4 3 2 1
First Edition

Random House Children's Books supports the First Amendment and celebrates the right to read.

Now You See Me...

by Tish Rabe

based on a television script
by Katherine Standford

illustrated by Christopher Moroney

Random House New York

Nick said, "It's vacation!
And we have all week
to play games and have fun.
Want to play hide-and-seek?"

"You count and I'll hide,"
Sally said. "And you'll see—
I'll hide so well that
you'll never find me!"

Sally looked till she found
a good hiding spot.
". . . Ten!" Nick called out.
"Coming! Ready or not!"

Where was Sally hiding?
In less than a minute,
Nick ran to the wheelbarrow
and found Sally in it!

"Hide-and-seek!" cried the Cat.

"Oh, I'm so glad I came!

The counting! The hiding!

It's my favorite game!"

"It's great!" Nick agreed.

Sally said as she sighed,

"But Nick always finds me

wherever I hide."

"Aha!" said the Cat.
"We must leave right away
to meet my friend Gecko,
who plays every day.

He hides in the day
and also at night.
It helps him stay safe
to keep out of sight."

So they flew to the jungle.

It was steamy and hot.

"My friend," said the Cat,

"is not easy to spot.

Cam-ou-flage helps him hide.

It is his hiding trick."

"Cam-ou-*what*? I don't know

what that word means!" said Nick.

"I'll explain," said the Cat. "Camouflage is the way some animals stay out of sight every day.

Camouflage helps them hide
so they will not be found.
It helps them blend in
with whatever's around."

"That Gecko blends in.
He's not easy to see."
"Hello!" Gecko called.
"Are you looking for me?
My tail looks leaf-like
and my skin is light brown.
I'm hanging right here in
this tree upside down!"

"Could you show us," asked Sally,

"how to hide like you do?

We want to learn how

to use camouflage too!"

"In the jungle," said Gecko,

"your clothes are too bright.

You need to blend in

so you stay out of sight."

"We can't hide dressed like this,"
said Nick. "What to do?"
"You need help," said the Cat,
"from Thing One and Thing Two!"
"Can you help us," asked Sally,
"look leafy and green?
If we look like the jungle,
we'll never be seen."

So, before the kids knew it,
they got a surprise—
Things One and Two made
them the perfect disguise!

"Mr. Gecko," said Nick,
"you can hide, it is true.
But can you find us
when we're hiding from *you*?"

"Of course!" Gecko said,
but when he looked around,
those camouflaged kids
were nowhere to be found!

He looked in the shadows
and looked in the light.
They were hiding so well
they were nowhere in sight.

Then all of a sudden
a tree started to wiggle.
"Wait!" Gecko said.
"I just heard someone giggle!
Out here in the jungle,"
he said with a smile,
"the trees haven't giggled
in quite a long while."

26

27

"Nick," Sally asked,
"when I was hiding today,
how did you find where
I was right away?"
"Well," Nick said, "finding
you wasn't hard.
Your dress was the only pink
thing in my yard."

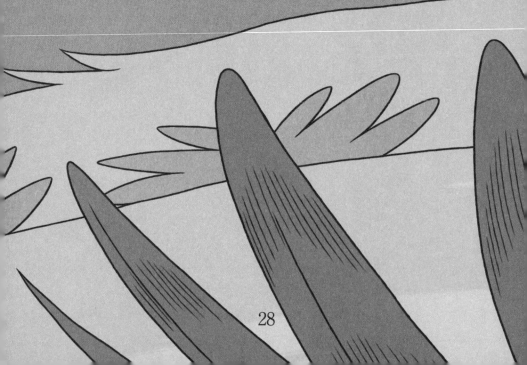

"Hide-and-seek," said the Cat,
"is so much fun to play.
I could play it with Gecko
and you every day.

But we have to go now.

We'll be back soon, I know.

Goodbye, Gecko!

Oh . . . Gecko?"

"NOW where did he go?"